Barrie

Sus

Methuen Drama

Published by Methuen Drama 2010

1 3 5 7 9 10 8 6 4 2

Methuen Drama
A & C Black Publishers Limited
36 Soho Square
London W1D 3QY
www.methuendrama.com

First published in 1979 by Eyre Methuen Ltd

ISBN 978 1 408 13137 4

A CIP catalogue record for this book is available from
the British Library

Typeset by MPS Limited, a Macmillan Company
Printed and bound in Great Britain by
CPI Cox & Wyman, Reading, Berkshire

A Young Vic and eclipse theatre co-production

Sus
by Barrie Keeffe

Sus opened at the Young Vic on 08 June 2010 after a tour that included Lincoln Performing Arts Centre, The Curve Leicester, The Broadway Barking, South Hill Park Bracknell, Birmingham Rep and Pulse Festival Ipswich.

Sus

by Barrie Keeffe

Karn **Simon Armstrong**
Delroy **Clint Dyer**
Wilby **Laurence Spellman**

Direction **Gbolohan Obisesan**
Set **Chloe Lamford**
Light **Anna Watson**
Sound **Donato Wharton**
Casting **Amy Ball**
Tour Marketing and Press **Jane Morgan Associates**
Production Manager **Andrew Quick**
Audience Development Officer **Bid Mosaku**
DSM **Kala Simpson**
Fight Director **Alison Deburg**
Workshop Leader **Vernon Douglas**

Originally produced as part of the Jerwood
Directors Award 2008, supported by Jerwood
Charitable Foundation.

Barrie Keeffe Playwright

Barrie was born in East London in 1945. He was an actor with the National Youth Theatre and a journalist before turning to full time dramatic writing and directing.

Theatre plays include: *A Mad World My Masters, Frozen Assets, Bastard Angel, King of England, Better Times, My Girl, Wild Justice* and two trilogies *Gimmer Shelter* (*Gem, Gotcha* and *Getaway*) and *Barbarians* (*Killing Time, Abide With Me* and *In The City*.) He also wrote the musical *Chrous Girls* with *Ray Davies*.

Screenplays and writing for television include: *The Long Good Friday, The Substitute, Not Quite Cricket, Gotcha, Nipper, Hanging Around, Waterloo Sunset, King* and the series *No Excuses*. He has written a dozen plays for BBC Radio and published two novels *Gadabout* and *No Excuses*. His adaptations for the theatre include *A Certain Vincent* (from the letters of van Gogh), Dostoyevsky's *A Gentle Spirit* and Le Compte de Lautreamont's *Maldoror* - these he directed in London and Amsterdam. Awards: The Mystery Writers of America Edgar Allen Poe Award for *The Long Good Friday*, Paris Critics Prix Revelation for *Gotcha* and the Giles Cooper Best Radio Plays Award for *Heaven Scent*.

He has taught dramatic writing at City University London, the Skyros Writers Lab, Greece and leads classes at the Collaldra Writers' School and Retreat near Venice each summer. He was Judith E. Wilson Fellow at Christ's College Cambridge 2003-4, is patron of Writing for Performance at Ruskin College Oxford and was made an Honorary Doctor of Letters at Warwick University earlier this year.

BIOGRAPHIES

Simon Armstrong Karn
Theatre includes: *To Kill a Mockingbird, One Flew Over the Cuckoo's Nest, Hobson's Choice, Of Mice and Men, Waiting for Godot* and *The Cherry Orchard* (all Clwyd Theatr Cymru where Simon is an Associate Actor); *Oleanna* and *Educating Rita* (Dukes Theatre Lancaster); *Antony and Cleopatra* and *Julius Caesar* (Shakespeare at the Tobacco Factory); *Troilus and Cressida* (Edinburgh International Festival and RSC); *Uncle Vanya* (Bristol Old Vic).
Film includes: *Pierrepoint - The Last Hangman* (Redbus Film Distribution/ IFC Films); *The Edge of Love* (BBC Films); *Dagenham Girls* (Number 9 Films).

Clint Dyer Delroy
Theatre include: *Big White Fog* (Almeida); *A Carpet, A Pony and A Monkey* (Bush Theatre); *It's A Big Shame* (Theatre Royal, Stratford East); *Hanging The President* (Traverse Theatre/BAC).
Film includes: *Unknown White Male* (Dark Castle Entertainment); *Agora* (MOD Films); *Bean II* (Working Title); *Portrait of London* (Red Mullet); *The Trail* (Gaumont); *Sahara* (Paramount); *Mr Inbetween* (Enterprise Films/ Lionsgate).
Television includes: *Hope Springs* (Shed Productions); *Fallout* (Company Pictures); *Trial and Retribution XII* (LaPlante Productions); *The Commander* (LaPlante Productions).

Laurence Spellman Wilby
Theatre includes: *The Gods Weep* (RSC); *Cyrano de Bergerac* (Chichester); *The Changeling, Cymbeline* and *Troilus & Cressida* (Cheek by Jowl/ Barbican/ Tour); *Kebab* (Royal Court); *Bent* (Trafalgar Studios); *Antony and Cleopatra* (Royal Exchange); *Charley's Aunt* (Exeter Northcott); *They Shoot Horses Don't They?* (National Youth Theatre, Apollo).
Television and Film includes: *The Tudors* (Showtime/BBC); *Small Island* (BBC); *Henry VIII: Mind of a Tyrant* (Channel 4); *The Bill* (ITV); *The Waltz King* (BBC); *The Libertine*.

Gbolahan Obisesan Direction
As director, theatre includes: *Eye/Balls* (Soho); *200 Years* (Watford Palace); *My Life* (Croydon Warehouse); *Excerpt of Tintin in Tibet* (Young Vic/Talawa); *Hold it Up* (Soho); *Skipping Rope* (Lowry Studio, Manchester); *Roadside* (Lyric Hammersmith Studio).
As assistant director for the Young Vic: *Generation, Impempe Yomlingo/ The Magic Flute & Ikrismas Kherol/A Christmas Carol.*
As assistant director, other theatre includes: *Death and the King's Horseman* (National Theatre); *Random, Alaska* (Royal Court); *Heat and Light* (Hampstead); *Astronaut Wives Club* and *3 Days in July* (Soho); *The Shipwrights' Tale* (NYT).

Anna Watson Light
Theatre, opera and dance include: *Soul Play* (Watford Palace Theatre); *My Zinc Bed* (Northampton Theatre Royal); *Ruddigore* (Opera North); *Plastic* (Victoria Baths, Manchester); *It Felt Empty When the Heart Went at First But It Is Alright Now* (Arcola Space K); *Rutherford and Son* (Northern Stage); *Something in the Air* (Contact, Manchester); *Twelfth Night* (Unicorn Theatre); *King Pelican* (Drum, Plymouth); *Salt* (Ruhr Triennale, Germany); *... Sisters* (Headlong); *Stumbling Over Infinity* (Linbury, Royal Opera House); *Critical Mass* (Almeida); *The Persian Revolution* (Lyric Hammersmith).

Donato Wharton Sound
Born in Cardiff on June 18th, 1976, Donato lived in Germany for 18 years, where he was based variously in Stuttgart, Cologne and Berlin. He lives and works in London as a musician and sound designer and has published three records on the Manchester/Berlin based label City Centre Offices. For the past two years he has worked as the Sound Manager on the European and North American Tours of the Robert Lepage/Ex machina production *Le Dragon Bleu (The Blue Dragon)*. Recent designs for theatre include *Sus* (Young Vic), *The Boy From Centreville* (Edinburgh Fringe Festival), *Back At You* (BAC), *The Body of Mr Smith* (Heidelberg/Germany). Donato trained at The Central School of Speech and Drama.

Chloe Lamford Design
Theatre and opera includes: *The Trial* (Gate Theatre); *Women on the Verge of HRT* (Derby Live); *Daisy Pulls it Off* and *Blythe Spirit* (Watermill Theatre); *It Felt Empty...* and *This Wide Night* (Clean Break); *The Kreutzer Sonata* (Gate Theatre); *Songs for a Hotel Bedroom* and *Soul Play*, both with Chor/Dir. Kate Flatt; *Everything Must Go* (Soho Theatre); *The Magic Flute* (English Touring Opera); *The Snow Queen* (Sherman Cymru); *War and Peace* (Royal Scottish Academy of Music and Drama/Scottish Opera); *The Cunning Little Vixen* (The Royal College of Music).
Film includes: *The Full Monteverdi* (Silicon 19); *The Four Dreams of Miss X* (Agent Provocateur) and a new play by Mark Ravenhill which will be produced in June at the Riverside Studios and will then be filmed by Sky Arts and broadcast live.

Stop and Search Form

Form Ref

Family name ....

First name(s) ....

Gender M • • F • • DoB [ ][ ][ ][ ][ ][ ][ ]   A/Age ....

IC Code [ ]   SDE Code [ ]   Height................Place of Birth ....

Address ....

....Post Code [ ][ ][ ][ ] [ ][ ][ ]

Vehicle Type ....VRM ....

Search Grounds ....

....

....

....

....

	Stop/Search	**Search (if different location)**
Date	[ ][ ][ ][ ][ ][ ][ ]	[ ][ ][ ][ ][ ][ ][ ]
Time	[ ][ ][ ][ ]	[ ][ ][ ][ ]

Loc'n ....

LPA ....Sector Code [ ][ ]   LPA....................Sector Code [ ][ ]

	Search Code [ ]	Outcome Code [ ]	Arrest Code [ ]

Person Y• •N• •Vehicle Y• •N• •Damage Caused*• •Injury Caused*• •Property Seized*• •

*Details..

Searching Officer..

Shoulder No. [ ][ ][ ][ ]   B(OCU)................Station Team/Unit....................

Copy of Person Searched

eclipse theatre

eclipse theatre has a mission to influence and instigate change that will lead to a more diverse and equitable theatrical landscape. By producing high quality middle scale touring work from a Black British perspective, eclipse theatre increases the diversity of work on offer to existing audiences whilst attracting new audiences. eclipse theatre aims to raise the profile of black theatre practitioners.

Since 2003, in partnership with a consortium of regional producing theatres, eclipse theatre has toured:

Moon on a Rainbow Shawl by Errol John, *Mother Courage and Her Children* by Bertolt Brecht, adapted by Oladipo Agboluaje, *Little Sweet Thing* by Roy Williams, *Three Sisters* by Anton Chekhov, adapted by Mustapha Matura *Angel House* by Roy Williams, (nomination for Best Actress in a visiting production MEN awards) *The Hounding of David Oluwale* by Kester Aspden, adapted by Oladipo Agboluaje (nominated for Best Director TMA awards)

Artistic Director **Dawn Walton**

eclipse theatre Is funded by the Arts Council of England.

For more information about eclipse theatre please visit www.eclipsetheatre.org.uk or join our Facebook Group

Little Sweet Thing

Mother Courage
and her Children

The Hounding of
David Oluwale

The Young Vic

'You really sense a special mood of open-mindedness at the Young Vic.'
Evening Standard

'Thank God for the Young Vic.'
The Observer

Our shows
We present the widest variety of classics, new plays, forgotten works and music theatre. We tour and co-produce extensively within the UK and internationally.

Our artists
Our shows are created by some of the world's great theatre people alongside the most adventurous of the younger generation.
This fusion makes the Young Vic one of the most exciting theatres in the world.

Our audience
... is famously the youngest and most diverse in London. We encourage those who don't think theatre is 'for them' to make it part of their lives. We give 10% of our tickets to schools and neighbours irrespective of box office demand, and keep prices low.

Our partners near at hand
Each year we engage with 10,000 local people – individuals and groups of all kinds including schools and colleges – by exploring theatre on and off stage. From time to time we invite our neighbours to appear on our stage alongside professionals.

Our partners further away
By co-producing with leading theatre, opera, and dance companies from around the world we challenge ourselves and create shows neither partner could achieve alone.

The Young Vic is a company limited by guarantee, registered in England No. 1188209
VAT Registration No. 236 673 348
The Young Vic (registered charity no. 268876) receives public funding from:

Supporting the Young Vic

The Young Vic relies on the generous support of many trusts, companies, and individuals to continue our work, on and off stage, year on year.

For their recent support we thank

Public Funders
Arts Council England
Lambeth Borough Council
London Development
Agency
Southwark Council

Corporate Supporters
American Airlines
Bupa
Bloomberg
De La Rue Charitable Trust
HSBC Bank plc
J.P. Morgan
KPMG Foundation
London Communications
Agency
North Square Capital
The Merlin Entertainment
London Eye

The Directors' Circle

Big Cheeses
HgCapital
Ingenious Media Plc
Land Securities

Hot Shots
Bloomberg
Clifford Chance
Slaughter and May
Taylor Wessing LLP

Trust Supporters
The Arimathea Charitable
Trust
The City Bridge Trust
City Parochial Foundation
John S Cohen Foundation
Columbia Foundation Fund
of the Capital Community
Foundation
Dorset Foundation
D'Oyly Carte Charitable
Trust

Equitable Charitable Trust
Eranda Foundation
Ernest Cook Trust
Esmée Fairbairn
Foundation
Foundation for Sport &
the Arts
Garrick Charitable Trust
Garfield Weston
Foundation
Genesis Foundation
Goethe-Institut
Gosling Foundation
Help a London Child
Henry Smith Charity
Jerwood Charitable
Foundation
John Ellerman Foundation
John Thaw Foundation
The Limbourne Trust
Man Group plc Charitable
Trust
Martin Bowley Charitable
Trust
Peter Moores Foundation
Quercus Charitable Trust
Steel Charitable Trust
The Worshipful Company
of Grocers
29th May 1961 Charitable
Trust

Production Partnership
Tony & Gisela Bloom
Sandy Chalmers
Kay Ellen Consolver &
John Storkerson
Eileen Glynn
Mr and Mrs Roderick Jack
Chris & Jane Lucas
Miles Morland
Nadine Majaro & Roger
Pilgrim
Anda & Bill Winters

Best Friends
Jane Attias
Chris & Frances Bates
Alex & Angela Bernstein
The Bickertons
Katie Bradford
Sarah Hall
Richard Hardman &
Family
Nik Holttum & Helen
Brannigan
Suzanne & Michael
Johnson
Tom Keatinge
John Kinder & Gerry
Downey
Carol Lake
Simon & Midge Palley
Naomi Russell
Charles & Donna Scott
Justin Shinebourne
Richard & Julie Slater
The Tracy Family
Leo & Susan van der
Linden
Rob Wallace

Great Friends
Angus Aynsley & Miel de
Botton Aynsley
Tim & Caroline Clark
Robyn Durie
Maureen Elton
Jenny Hall
Susan Hyland
Tony Mackintosh
Ian McKellen
Barbara Minto
Frank & Helen Neale
Georgia Oetker
Richard Tompkins and
Kirsten Lass
Donna & Richard Vinter
Jimmy & Carol Walker

Giving a voice to young talent

Land Securities is proud to sponsor the Young Vic

LandSecurities

Sus

For Harvey Unna

List of characters

Karn
Wilby
Delroy

Music:

Before the play: Bob Dylan's 'Hurricane' from the album *Desire*

Before Acts Two and Three: Bob Dylan's 'Baby Stop Crying' from the album *Street Legal*

After the play: Bob Marley's 'No Woman No Cry' from the album *Live*

Lyrics quoted in Act Two 'No Woman No Cry' by Bob Marley copyright © Rondor Music Ltd

Introduction

There's a quote of mine that has come to haunt me because it so frequently and often inappropriately turns up. I once said to a journalist (and I clearly recall saying it): 'I write plays for people who wouldn't be seen dead in a theatre.' My agent at the time, the now late Harvey Unna, shook his head in wry disbelief when he saw it in the newspaper and said, 'Frankly Barrie, with those thirteen ill-chosen words you have done untold damage to your career – what theatre will ever want your plays now?' I knew exactly what he meant but there had been a very apt reason for saying what I said. It was because of this play *Sus*.

I wrote the play shortly after Margaret Thatcher was swept to power in May 1979 and told the world from the steps of 10 Downing Street: 'Where there is discord may we bring harmony. Where there is despair may we bring hope.' Living in South East London at the time where the British Fascists were causing fear and havoc I felt very little hope and wrote the play quickly.

The story of the miscarriage and death of an Anglo-Caribbean woman and the police's immediate suspicion and grievous mistreatment of her husband was a true story I had covered in the mid-'sixties while working as a reporter on a local weekly newspaper in East London. However, it wasn't until Mrs Thatcher took up the reins that I found the necessary backdrop for the play by setting it on election night and the 'new dawn,' as Karn chillingly calls it. When the soft gloves of restraint came off.

I originally used the medical term 'A Rare Complication' as the title for the play but Verity Bargate, who ran the Soho Poly where it, like seven other of my plays, was originally staged immediately changed the title to *Sus*, arguing, irrefutably, that one word titles were cheaper to advertise in *The Guardian* theatre listings. It proved an excellent choice, as was her decision to switch the schedules

and rush forward the opening to within six weeks of Mrs
Thatcher becoming Prime Minister. Ann Mitchell's
production struck an immediate nerve and the tiny theatre
with just thirty-five seats started playing three shows a day
with often an audience of more than a hundred standing.

The production moved onto the Royal Court Theatre
and, after a series of one-night stands in libraries and social
clubs for the Stop Sus campaign, was summoned by Philip
Hedley to the Theatre Royal, Stratford East, when he
became Artistic Director that autumn. It was greeted with
great excitement from predominantly black houses and
Paul Barber frequently had to remind the angry audiences
in the bar afterwards that Stuart Barren, playing Karn, *was
an actor and not a racist cop* for Stuart's safety. This scenario
was repeated when John McGarth's 7:84 Company toured
Britain for several months later that year.

None of this matched the extraordinary nights ten years
later when *Sus* was staged at the Greenwich Theatre shortly
after the racist murder of teenager Stephen Lawrence in
nearby Eltham. On stage for three nights after the show
Stephen's parents and the local police debated the killing
and the subsequent investigation with extreme noise and
agitation from passionate audiences who stressed to me just
how vital theatre's value can be in our present society.

Now back to the 'I write plays for people who wouldn't
be seen dead in a theatre' quip. I very clearly remember
saying this during a Rock Against Racism concert in a field
outside Oxford on August Bank Holiday Monday 1979.
Many thousands had gathered and we, who had been
asked to perform our play, doubted many would stay to see
the play that night before the headliners Misty. The three
actors needed individual hand-held microphones rather
like the Supremes or the Four Tops to 'reach out' to the
vast audience that *did* stay with the play which began as the
sun went down. As twilight settled we apprehensively
realised that the entire gathering had been surrounded by

a huge ring of uniformed police on the outer perimeter of the field, presumably anticipating trouble that never came.

The ovation at the end of the play lasted a long time and the bands back-stage had stayed to watch and led the applause. I was incredibly surprised and moved by the entire experience and so was off-guard when the journalist reminded me he'd once interviewed me about another play at the Soho Poly that had gotten lousy audiences. 'Surprisingly good crowd for your play here in Oxford today,' he said with a kind of smirk. 'How many thousands do they reckon?' That's when I made the mistake of joking about 'plays for people who wouldn't be seen dead in a theatre.'

I hadn't anticipated that *Sus* would prove equally popular in theatres around the world – it has played New York twice, Los Angeles and several other US cities as well as Europe and Australia. It has also been seen in Pakistan and India both in the version in this text but also in adaptations taking in similar local situations. I'm surprised and rather saddened that a play I wrote thirty-one years ago and thought then was, as one critic described it, a piece of 'instant political theatre' – implying it had no longevity – actually still does have a painful resonance and not just to theatre audiences. As I write this a film version is playing the festival circuit before national and international cinema release. (www.susthemovie.om)

Maybe I should change the title: instead of *Sus* (Suspect Under Suspicion) call it *Sas* (Stop and Search). Of course, paying due respect to Section 44 of the Terrorism Act of 2000 . . .

Barrie Keeffe
London, April 2010

Act One

Stark interview room; a table and two upright chairs.

Enter **Karn** *with a paper cup of coffee.*

He clears cigarette ends from the table, empties the ashtray, sits, lights a cigarette, checks his watch, waits.

Enter **Wilby**, *younger.*

Wilby   He's here.

Karn   Any results in yet?

Wilby   I haven't heard.

Karn   Glasgow's first, isn't it?

Wilby   I believe.

Karn   We could do with a portable telly.

Wilby   They've got one downstairs.

Karn   In here, I mean.

Wilby   We could keep popping down.

Karn   BBC or ITN?

Wilby (*laughs*)   Anna Ford.

Karn   Snotty little cow. I wouldn't mind giving her one. Her interview with the Thatch. I thought they both came out of it rather well.

Wilby   Woman Prime Minister?

Karn   Her heart's in the right place. Even if her brains are up her arsehole.

Wilby   We shouldn't be too long, should we?

Karn   You've seen him! Election night. A new dawn. I don't want to welcome in that on the job. What's he like?

Wilby   Bit tatty.

Karn   Talks English?

Wilby   I can understand him.

Karn   Anything on him?

Wilby   No form at all.

Karn   Maybe I should take a look . . .

Wilby   He's in the –

Karn   What time is the Thorpe result?

Wilby   Pardon?

Karn   That's the one that intrigues me . . .

Wilby   Not 'til about four or five. If there's a recount.

Karn   A what?

Wilby   A recount.

Karn   This must be the only country in the world where a bloke on a murder charge can stand for Parliament. If he's sent down, they'll bung him in the Cabinet. Fucking Liberals.

Wilby   His name's Delroy, Leon.

Karn   And you picked him up?

Wilby   Boozer at the bottom of his road. The hospital casualty doctor phoned the nick at eight thirty – no sign of Delroy at his flat, a neighbour said the boozer and we picked him up there.

Karn   Fuss?

Wilby   He just laughed.

Karn   He what?

Wilby   Laughed.

Karn   Bit fucking naff. Wife dying in a pool of blood and he –

Wilby   He ain't mentioned her.

Karn Not a word?

Wilby He hasn't denied nothing neither.

Karn There's grief. So what's he think we've picked him up for then?

Wilby Sus.

Karn Sus?

Wilby I reckon he thinks it's sus.

Karn And he didn't make no racket, no screaming his rights or –

Wilby No.

Karn He must have been picked up on sus a few times then.

Wilby He's the sort of geezer you would. I don't like the look of his beard.

Karn Any form?

Wilby No convictions. He's had his dabs taken a few times.

Karn It's coming to something then –

Wilby Eh?

Karn Pick a bloke up so often on sus he don't even notice it. Ought to fit him up now and again, to relieve the fucking monotony for him.

Wilby I'll check again.

Karn Yeah. Aliases. Who's round his drum?

Wilby Charlie and Harry are rolling it now. Susie went and all. Three youngsters. Waiting social services. Put them in care 'til . . . sorted out.

Karn Good. Want a bet on the result?

Wilby The doctors said –

Karn   I mean, the election?

Wilby   Oh.

Karn   Majority of how many?

Wilby   Twenty five?

Karn   You're on. Pony?

Wilby   You reckon more?

Karn   Tory landslide.

Wilby   A pony then.

Karn *lights a cigarette.*

Karn   A woman bleeds to death and her old man's in the boozer enjoying himself . . .

Pause.

What time are they doing the post-mortem?

Wilby   Doctors are off now. Earliest'll be nine in the morning.

Karn   Can we charge him 'til then?

Wilby   Doctors are positive. Massive haemorrhage. Harry's throwing up over the bed sheets, nightdress smothered and –

Karn   Cunt. I'll have the nightie.

Wilby   The nightie?

Karn   Might break him down if he's feigning. Know what I mean?

Wilby   Right.

Karn   Wheel him in then. I didn't get to be in the position I am today by wasting time. And I want to be home in time to toast in the new dawn. Book him first.

Wilby   I'll wheel him in then.

Wilby *goes.* **Karn** *goes to the phone (which is not on the desk).*

Karn   Dave listen, as soon as Harry and Charlie get back let me have a word with them, right. Any results in yet? Labour fucking winning seats! Oh well, Scottish Nationalists! They don't count.

He replaces receiver as **Wilby** *enters with* **Delroy**. *Pause.*

Delroy   We ain't been introduced. My name is Leon Delroy.

Karn   How very civilised Mr Delroy. How very nice to make your acquaintance. D.C. Wilby and me, D.S. Karn.

Delroy   Well, well – this is a nice room. I haven't been in this room before.

Karn   Décor's quite simple. Let me show you around. We've gone in for the hardwearing but easy to clean.

Delroy   Do you get a lot of mess in here then?

Karn   You never can tell.

Delroy   Very nice. Very, um, simple.

Karn   Same with the furniture. I trust you approve?

Delroy   Well I . . . what did you say your name was?

Karn   Karn. K A R N.

Delroy   Is that German or something?

Karn   It's my father's name. His father gave it to him and he gave it to me. Sort of family heirloom.

Delroy   Nice.

Karn   Handed down from generation to generation. All English. Pure stock.

Delroy   Well, this looks the most comfortable chair.

Karn   Then sit down, do sit down Mister Delroy. Take the weight off your feet. How long did you say you were in the boozer?

Delroy   From about sevenish.

Karn   More than three hours solid boozing! Then my gawdfathers, you must be fucking worn out Mister Delroy. I do apologise. Perhaps, Wilby, you could bring in a chaise-longue to make Mister Delroy here a bit more comfortable.

Delroy   You're too kind, Mister Karn, but this'll do. As it happens, I haven't got too much time to spare tonight. I'm in a bit of a hurry. We're going down to the club to watch the election results.

Karn   The club, eh? What one's that? Beefsteak? Brooks? White's or the M.C.C.?

Delroy (*laughing*)   I ain't fussy.

Karn   That's nice to hear.

Delroy   As it happens, Working Men's Club. But if you was thinking of inviting me to one of them –

Karn   Actually, I wasn't. Working Men's Club, you say . . . if you don't mind me asking Mister Delroy, what exactly do you work at. Profession?

Delroy   Well, Mister Karn, to tell you the truth, it's a period of readjustment I'm into now.

Karn   I see. How do you mean, exactly?

Delroy   I'm sort of . . . re-assessing the situation. I'm thinking maybe I won't concentrate on being a C.L.O. after all –

Karn   Really? That sounds a most fascinating field of work.

Delroy   To tell you the truth, although it sounds glamorous –

Karn   Glamorous, yes –

Delroy   It ain't. In fact, being a –

Karn   Capstan lathe operator –

Delroy   To tell you the truth, it's a bit fucking boring. So for the last eighteen months –

Karn   You gave up the job?

Delroy   More, it gave me up. So me and the Job Centre, like we've got to concentrating on not doing nothing. You know, it's a pretty fucking democratic arrangement. They do fuck all for me and I do fuck all for them.

Pause. He has rolled a cigarette.

Could I trouble you for a light?

Karn   You're not seriously proposing to smoke a cigarette and not offer one to me and Mister Wilby, are you?

Delroy   Here's the baccy, here's the skins.

Karn   After all the hospitality we've given you – chair, feet up, tinkle of tea cups . . . you might as least roll us one apiece.

Delroy (*laughing*)   Well, to tell you the truth . . . I had a dose a little while back and –

Karn   From a lavatory seat?

Delroy   I reckon, another geezer's spittle –

Karn   No wonder they prohibit gobbing on lav seats.

Delroy (*laughing*)   Yeah, right – a dose, see and –

Wilby   A dose? (*Pause.*) You think that's funny?

Pause

Delroy   I thought it would be all right to mention it here, in confidence, no ladies present, are there?

Karn   Talking of ladies!

Delroy   I didn't know we was?

Karn   I bet you're a ladies' man, Mister Delroy.

Delroy Oh yeah? (*He laughs.*)

Karn Are you a Ford or a Rippon man?

Delroy Eh?

Karn Anna Ford or Angela Rippon?

Delroy Oh . . .

Karn Election results. BBC or ITN?

Delroy I see what you mean.

Karn Well?

Delroy Well, that's a bit tricky. That's a hell of a decision. Whatever's on at the club, you know.

Wilby On occasions. It's an occasion after all.

Delroy Oh yeah, on occasions I like to be loyal.

Karn BBC?

Delroy Cup Final, always I watch BBC.

Karn And tonight?

Delroy Well, Anna – know what I mean? Sorry, but I think Anna'll get my vote.

He laughs a lot.

Get my vote – election, like. Get it?

Karn How very droll. Poor old Angela.

Delroy Oh, don't tempt me with Angela, Mister Karn. It's too much. I couldn't cope with that. Spare me that. Spare me that decision.

Karn I sympathise. I understand.

Delroy Like, I come home from collecting the dole, right? Like I get £23.57 for three kids and me wife, now she's got another one on the way and she don't work and . . . four of us and a baby living off £23.57 –

Karn Come off it, the extras must double that easy.

Delroy I'm talking about the dole. A few extras, but they won't even pay me gas bill for me.

Karn What do I pay my taxes for?

Delroy Final demand £35.23. They're gonna cut me off. Well, coming home with all them problems, like –

Karn You come into your flat, right. Wife and kids are out. You look in one bedroom and there's Anna Ford: stark naked, legs open, on the bed, waiting for you.

Pause.

In the other bedroom, there's Angela Rippon: not a stitch on, wetting herself for you.

Delroy Yeah?

Karn One, only one. What one do you choose?

Pause.

Delroy How do I know they want me?

Karn They tell you?

Delroy Really?

Karn Which one?

Delroy Both!

Karn Which one first, though?

Delroy Hmmm.

He concentrates.

Only one? You sure?

Karn One.

Delroy Hmmmmmmmm.

Karn Well, which?

Pause.

Delroy   This is a very difficult decision for me to have to make.

Karn   Of course it is.

Delroy   I ain't used to having to make decisions like this.

Karn   Get a move on, they won't be there forever.

Delroy   Can I have time to think?

Karn   Snap decision. Be spontaneous.

Delroy   Well, see, thinking it through . . . I come up the stairs. Depends who I see first. Like, if I see Anna first . . . I mean, she really is a very sexy little lady. And clean. You can see that. I reckon she takes a lot of time and trouble cleaning herself up. And her mouth. Goes like, you know how her mouth goes whenever that drunk bloke burps or farts or something, you know. (*He impersonates her.*) I reckon she's a fantastic blow-job chick.

Karn   So Anna Ford?

Delroy   Don't rush me! I might not get this chance again. See, if I clock Angela Rippon like . . . bit of class, her eyebrows, you know. (*He does an eyebrow impersonation.*) Like, innocent but . . . them bints, always look like butter wouldn't melt in their cunts but –

Karn   So?

Delroy   Oh, shit man. Like, I been on the dole a year and a half. I do shit jobs when I work. Like, I only get 24 quid a week and . . . I ain't even got no decent clothes or nothing and . . . we ain't got a lav to ourselves and . . . I couldn't get it on with Anna or Angela in my rooms. Anyway! We share one bedroom. We only got one bedroom.

Karn   One?

Delroy   You said there's Anna in one and Angela in the other –

Karn   Right –

Delroy   But we've only got one bedroom.

Karn   Make out you've got two.

Delroy   Come off it, I ain't a genius. I ain't no Mastermind of imagination. It's pretty fucking hard imagining Angela Rippon and Anna Ford both want me to fuck the arse off them without –

Wilby   What would your wife say?

Pause.

Delroy   What?

Wilby   Your wife. How would she feel – what would she say? When she hears you're knocking them off?

Delroy   What, if she hears I'm having wild sex orgies with two TV newsreaders?

Wilby   How would your wife react?

Delroy   Well . . . (*pause*) I think she'd be a bit fucking amazed.

Wilby   You'd tell her then?

Delroy   Listen man, if I come home and them two are lying stark cunt naked waiting for me to chuck me cock – I'd dial a phone-in and tell the whole fucking world.

Wilby   A lot of wives would be deeply hurt. (*Pause.*) They'd feel betrayed.

Delroy   Yeah, sure. I mean, sure. I mean, once she got over the shock, like.

Wilby   She'd be deeply wounded, I'd say.

Delroy   She'd be a bit put out, in case I left her. To go and live in Knightsbridge with one of them, sure.

Wilby   You don't have very much respect for your wife's feelings then, do you?

Delroy   I got a lot of respect for her, a lot – a hell of a lot.
But I mean, this is a bit special like. This don't happen
every day. Like if Mick Jagger was chucking his cock at her,
I'd be a bit of a mean bastard to tell her to tell him to fuck
off with his millions, like.

Karn   Now, now Mister Wilby. I mean, we are being
hypothetical aren't we. (*To* **Delroy**, *confidentially.*) D.C. Wilby,
he's a very moral man.

Delroy   I'm a moral man and all. I mean – on 24 quid a
week I haven't got much choice.

Karn   Not exactly bombarded with temptation then?

Delroy   No. (*To* **Wilby**.) Look, don't have a go for dirty talk
at me. He started it. I thought it was leading up to him
getting me pants off and measuring me prick or something.
I was just going along with him like. I didn't like it, like.

Karn   Things you don't like . . . are you a man who can
resist temptation?

Pause

Delroy   I go for a good crap and think of England.

Pause. Then **Karn** *laughs heartily and pats* **Delroy**'s *shoulder.*

Karn   You know, I think I'm going to like you Mister
Delroy. Let's have a cup of coffee. Cup of coffee?

Delroy   Well, all right.

Karn   Three coffees, Wilby.

Wilby *goes, closing the door.*

Karn   Mister Delroy, sorry about that. Mister Wilby – he's a
moral man. He's very religious, really. I think he might
leave the force and take up the church. Priest or something.
He's always quoting the Bible – off duty. He's her . . . he's
very moral.

Delroy   Oh.

Karn Didn't appreciate our suppositions then.

Delroy Well, like I said – you started the dirty talk.

Karn My fault, my responsibility. Just for a laugh. You like a good laugh?

Delroy Yeah.

Karn A popular man. I can see you're a popular man. The sort of man whose company is desired.

Delroy Cops desire it.

Karn Really?

Delroy I seem to have something, you know. Like a chemical aroma. Attracts police to me. They cluster around me. They like to pass their time chatting me up. It's crazy.

Karn You're too sociable, perhaps.

Delroy Ah, I don't ask them. They come to me.
In fact, I've been known to try and keep out of their way but it seems like right now I can't walk down a road or wait at a bus stop or go for a drink without I get picked up by cops.

Karn It must be your personality.

Delroy If you don't mind me saying –

Karn What's that?

Delroy Confidentially, like –

Karn Your secrets are safe with me.

Delroy I mean, I wouldn't like you to think I'm complaining –

Karn I can see you're not that sort of man.

Delroy Well, they like to talk to me more than I like to talk to them. They even have to make up little lies to get my . . . attention.

Karn   Yes?

Delroy   Sus.

Karn   Oh!

Delroy   Suspicion of this, suspicion of that –

Karn   I've heard about it –

Delroy   Last month – this was all in three weeks, like – well
. . . At a bus stop they said I was loitering to dip an old
lady's handbag. It got chucked out of court, the magistrates
chucked it out. No witnesses. The very next day in the park,
they say they want me for possession of drugs. Then they
find I ain't got none so they say I'm a pusher and have
flogged them. I was in here for four hours. My old lady was
worried out of her head. Fat copper, got me pants off and
sticking his boot up me arse, said in case I'd hid them there.
The Law Centre said I could have sued you coppers for
something. Then picked up in the market on a Saturday
morning – bundled into the patrol car. They said they was
looking for a banana thief. 'I ain't got no bananas.' He said,
'Then we'll do you for motors or houses, you choose.' I said,
'I ain't particular.' Then they just let me go.

Karn *shakes his head and sighs.*

Karn   Very time consuming.

Delroy   I got a lot of spare time, but this is fucking
ridiculous.

Karn   Look on the bright side, you still haven't been
convicted.

Delroy   There's never been no fucking crime to convict me
for. Never no witnesses, never no evidence, never no
fucking crime.

Karn   Temper, temper.

Delroy   I never lose me temper.

Karn Wise. With policemen.

Delroy Lose your temper with a cop, that's assault. They lose their temper with you, it's called resisting arrest.

Karn Just a game of semantics.

Delroy I got witnesses.

Karn Witnesses?

Delroy That I ain't done nothing.

Karn How's that? I mean, how does anyone witness nothing?

Delroy Listen, I got references. I tell them to go and see my last boss. Reason he got the sack for me was, he said, 'Delroy, you lazy fucking nigger, you never do nothing.' (*Laughs.*) I should have asked him to write that down. (*Laughs.*) I should have got that in writing. To show people. Show cops like you.

Wilby *enters with three coffees in paper cups.*

Wilby Labour's lost three seats.

Karn Double milk in the coffees.

Wilby Anna Ford –

Karn Watch it.

Wilby She had a diagram. Said this could mean a Tory landslide.

Karn What did I tell you? What did I tell you? Sugar, Mister Delroy?

Delroy Matter of fact, if you've finished, I wouldn't mind going.

Karn Going? I mean, a man as responsible as you . . . going? We're about to celebrate. The beloved Thatch. I mean, you don't *want* to go, do you?

Delroy Well, I've got a confession to make. I'm not
a Tory.

Karn You're what?

Delroy I ain't Tory.

Pause.

Karn Has the issue of law and order not engaged you,
Mister Delroy?

Delroy Well, in my personal experience, like I was
explaining. Mister Karn, there ain't much order to law.
Know what I mean?

Karn What do you make of that, Mister Wilby?

Wilby That?

Karn What he said.

Wilby It sounded a bit . . .

Karn A bit?

Wilby Definitely out of order.

Karn I'm sure he didn't intend it to sound that way. Did
you Mister Delroy? Didn't intend to besmirch the men in
blue? No-one seems to realise except the Thatch, how
under strength we are, you know. Crime rising, fewer cops,
underpaid. I should be on sick leave.

Delroy I worked it out.

Pause.

Karn What did he say?

Wilby I think he said –

Karn What?

Wilby He said, he's worked it out.

Karn What have you worked out, Mister Delroy?

Delroy   Well . . . (*Pause.*) I think you've got a problem. I've seen it, with me own eyes. And having given it some consideration, I reckon . . .

Karn   Tell me.

Delroy   If you spend less time harassing people who ain't done nothing, you'd have a lot more fucking time to spend chasing the bastards who have done crimes. That's what I think.

Karn   Must keep the streets safe for decent people.

Delroy   That's kids. I'm a married man, family man. So, if you don't mind, I'm going now. Just sus, right? Pick up some other fucking nigger. Fun over. I'm going. No crime so –

He goes towards the open door. **Karn** *leans back on the door, closing it.*

Karn   Actually Mister Delroy, there has been a crime tonight.

Pause.

Delroy   You must come across a lot in your job.

Karn   We do, oh we do.

Delroy   I'm going. OK. So if you'll excuse me . . .

Karn   You can't go.

Pause

Delroy   Why should I stay? I got my rights.

Karn   After all, you are involved.

Delroy   I'm what?

Karn   Tell him –

Wilby   You're involved.

Delroy   How's that then? Listen, I was in the pub from just after seven. I got witnesses. Before that I was at home. We got this problem with the fire and my old lady, 'cause she's

not too well, she's cold all the time, so I was fixing the gas
fire in the bedroom and –

Wilby   Are you qualified for such technical work? Gas is
specialised.

Delroy   It weren't working and the Gas Board wouldn't
come –

Wilby   Wouldn't come?

Delroy   When I phoned them up, they said you
have to book up for things if they ain't emergencies.
They said they couldn't come and I said my wife was
ill and they said maybe if one of the blokes felt like
a bit of –

Wilby   Wife not well, you say. Ill?

Delroy   Not too well. Having a few upsets. The pregnancy.
You know. She had it before. She stays in bed a lot and –

Wilby   And you went out, leaving her ill in bed?

Pause

Well, I mean to say, that was a bit callous, weren't it?

Delroy   The boys, the election and . . . It's OK. I put the
kids to bed before I came out and I'll check she's OK before
I go to the club. Any problem, she bangs on the floor and
the kid downstairs, he comes in the boozer and tells me and
two minutes later I'm back there, OK?

Pause. **Karn** *sits.*

Karn   So you last saw her . . . when did you last see her?

Delroy   When I got to the pub. Just before then.
Sevenish.

Pause.

Karn   What was she wearing?

Delroy   Eh?

Karn What was your wife wearing when you left her five hours ago.

Silence.

Delroy She was in bed.

Wilby Wearing?

Delroy What do you mean . . . wearing?

Wilby Describe what she was wearing?

Delroy Well, she was wearing this nightie thing, like.

Karn Like what?

Delroy Like, sort of, down here and . . . long and . . . kinda made her feel nice 'cause she weren't feeling too great and it was a bit cold, like she was and –

Karn Colour?

Delroy Colour? What do you mean colour?

Wilby Colour of the nightdress.

Pause.

Delroy Well, pink weren't it. Kinda pinkish and with white lacey bits round here and . . . no sleeves . . . she looked really good in it, you know, to cheer herself up, she looked really pretty, you know.

Karn Wilby, would you get the –

Wilby Of course.

Wilby *goes.*

Delroy I'll be off now and all –

Karn I'm afraid not, Mister Delroy. You see, there has been a crime tonight. This ain't sus.

Delroy Yeah well, it ain't nothing to do with me 'cause I got witnesses that I weren't nowhere except –

Karn   Sit down, Mister Delroy.

Delroy   You've got nothing on me, I'm going home –

Karn   Sit down, Mister Delroy.

Delroy   Go fuck yourself, I'm going –

He goes to the door: it opens and **Wilby** *enters carrying a plastic specimen bag. Pause.* **Delroy** *doesn't move.* **Wilby** *takes the bag to* **Karn**, *who looks in it. He looks at* **Delroy**. **Wilby** *stands in the doorway.*

Karn   She died tonight.

Pause.

At eight fifteen . . . your wife died.

Karn *stares at* **Delroy**.

There was a great loss of blood. In fact, once we get the post-mortem result, I wouldn't be surprised to hear that she bled to death.

Silence. Then **Delroy** *tries to laugh.*

Delroy   Very good . . . very good . . . bit fucking cruel, bit sadistic, know what I mean. I ain't done nothing. My wife ain't . . . How can you say such an evil thing? What you trying to fucking fit me up for? Me confess to robbing gas meters or something, that what you want, you cunt.

Karn   What was she wearing?

Delroy   I told you.

Karn   Mister Wilby, open the door.

Pause. Then **Wilby** *opens the door.* **Delroy** *hesitates.*

Delroy   You're crazy, you know that? Crazy. That's . . . vicious, what you said.

Karn   As you like.

Delroy   So I go then . . . OK? That's right then, I'm going, out of this madhouse – I'm off.

Karn   Oh, one thing Mister Delroy –

Delroy *stops at the open door and looks at* **Karn**.

If you'd just have a look . . . if this was the nightie your late wife was wearing.

Pause. **Karn** *tosses the plastic bag to* **Wilby**, *who opens it in front of* **Delroy**. *Pause.*

Mind the blood stains. Still warm, almost.

Delroy *looks in the bag. Silence. The phone rings.* **Karn** *lifts the receiver.*

Karn (*listens, then to* **Wilby**)   ITN predicting a 65 per cent majority . . . for the Thatch. (*He replaces the receiver.*) Sit down Delroy. Few things I want to ask you.

Delroy *looks at* **Karn**.

Oh yeah, she's dead.

Black out.

Music loud: chorus of Bob Dylan's 'Baby Stop Crying'.

Act Two

Delroy *sits at the table in silence.*

As music fades, enter **Wilby** *with one paper cup of coffee. He sits, lights a cigarette, sips the coffee, opens his notebook and takes out a biro.*

Pause. He looks at **Delroy**.

Wilby   Mister Delroy, there's no need for all that. I mean, it won't bring her back.

Pause. **Delroy** *begins to cry.*

You can't bring the dead back. I know about death. I have known people to die. I have even known the grief of a dog dying. Oh, that was terrible. Made worse by my feeling that somehow I shared the responsibility.

Pause.

Eight fifteen. Actually, she screamed a great deal. The Gas Board man fortunately arrived after all. Entered the premises to attend to the broken gas fire. He heard her screaming. Your children were extremely distressed. Well, that stands to reason, I suppose. That feeling of helplessness. I know that feeling. When the dog I was speaking of died, I felt extremely helpless. For children it must be . . . inconceivable. The Gas Board man did the right thing; he called an ambulance. The doctors at the hospital, they said it was too late. Oh, they examined her, they did their . . . business. But they were helpless with regard to arresting the approach of death, unfortunately. She died at eight fifteen.

Delroy   Oh God . . .

Wilby   Someone said . . . I recall hearing someone say . . . that death is worse for those who survive the death. I think that might well be the case. One can't confirm it with the dead.

Pause. **Wilby** *lights another cigarette and smoothes out his notebook on the table. Poised biro.*

Mister Karn is having his tea in the canteen. His
supper, I mean. He's watching the election programme
on TV. He hopes we can deal with all this without
disturbing him.

Pause.

Shall we begin at the beginning then?

Delroy   My kids . . . my kids . . . ?

Wilby   They're all right.

Delroy   They were there and . . .

Wilby   They're in care.

Delroy   What?

Wilby   Social services, for the night, put them into a hostel.
Well, two actually. They're being looked after. We arranged
it all very promptly.

Pause.

Wilby   We're used to dealing with unusual situations.

Delroy   I got to see them –

Wilby   Oh, that isn't possible.

Delroy   They need me –

Wilby   I beg your pardon?

Delroy   Time like this, they need their father, not some
fucking social workers –

Wilby   The time they needed their father he was drinking
in a pub. The time your wife and their mother died, you
were drinking in the pub. It appears the death was
extraordinarily painful. As one might imagine given the
unusual circumstances.

Pause.

Delroy   I can't believe she's dead.

Wilby   You must face the truth.

Delroy   I can't . . . believe it. Her . . . dying.

Wilby   Would you like to see the nightgown again?

Pause.

Delroy *begins to weep again.*

Now, that isn't helping anyone.

Delroy   I can't believe . . . can't . . . believe . . .

Pause.

Wilby   In times of extreme emotional crisis . . . it's often advisable to occupy the mind. So if we can establish the following facts. Yes? Do try to concentrate. Her full name?

Delroy   Whose?

Wilby   The deceased's.

Delroy   Georgie. I mean, Georgina. I called her Georgie.

Wilby   With a Y or an IE?

Pause. **Delroy** *stares at* **Wilby**.

Y or IE?

Delroy   I well, I never wrote it down.

Wilby   Never wrote down her name?

Delroy   When I wrote her name down I wrote Georgina.

Wilby   Georgina, then. (*He writes this down.*) And her age?

Delroy   She was . . . twenty . . . err . . . nine.

Wilby   She had two children –

Delroy   No, three.

Wilby   We can't include the aborted foetus as a child. Not in the file.

Delroy   We had three kids. We were going to have . . . four.

Pause.

Wilby   Names, dates of birth.

Delroy   Now?

Wilby   What do you mean, now?

Delroy   Listen, you've just told me my wife has died and –

Wilby   That is why we require all these details.

Delroy   I don't . . . don't know where my head is . . .

Wilby   It's in the usual place.

Delroy   Mean, my state of mind.

Wilby   Do you have a history of mental disorder?

Delroy   I never had a wife die before.

Wilby   First wife? Only one?

Delroy   Yeah, the only one.

Wilby   I see. (*He writes this down.*)

Delroy   Have you no . . . pity? My wife . . . all my adult life with this lady and –

Wilby   Years of marriage?

Delroy   I err . . . I was . . . twenty . . .

Wilby   How old was she?

Delroy   She was younger.

Wilby   Of legal age to marry?

Delroy   What do you mean?

Wilby   In this country, a bride must be sixteen.

Delroy   In this . . . country . . . we got married.

Pause.

Wilby   I see. Offspring: Names, dates of birth.

Delroy   Oh Christ.

Wilby   You can't have forgotten.

Delroy   'Course I haven't forgotten. Just . . . in the middle of . . . this confusion and this –

Wilby   The eldest.

Delroy   He's . . . Joey. He's eight. So he was born . . . June the err . . . on the . . . June the . . . 14th.

Wilby   You don't sound very certain.

Delroy   I'm certain. I'm . . . just not certain of the year.

Wilby   The year of birth of your eldest son?

Delroy   I'm a bit . . . in a bit of a state.

Wilby   But it seems a very simple question.

Delroy   He'll be eight on June 14th.

Wilby   Born in 1971, then?

Delroy   Yeah, the year Ali . . . um . . . the year –

Wilby   Were you his father?

Delroy   Eh?

Wilby   Only you don't seem very sure of the date of his birth; some mental block perhaps?

Delroy   'Course I'm his father. Listen, what the fuck, mister? What the fuck you meaning, what are you getting at, what the fuck is all this –

Wilby   Try to remain calm, Mister Delroy!

Pause.

I'm only doing my job.

He stares at **Delroy**, *then turns the page of his notebook.*

I don't want to be here on a murder case tonight. Now the names and –

Delroy   What?

Wilby   The other's children's names and dates of –

Delroy   Murder? How she die? What are you saying, eh?

Wilby   The circumstances of the death are extremely irregular. The doctors alerted us to the probability of foul play. Which will be confirmed in the post-mortem. That is why –

Delroy   You think . . . think someone killed her?

Wilby   Oh yes.

Pause.

Delroy   Who?

Silence. **Wilby** *makes some notes.*

I said –

Wilby   Must get all the details down.

Delroy   For God's sake, listen. Listen to me. To me. You hear me? You see me? I am . . . bleeding. Inside I am bleeding, man. I been here for an hour before you even tell me . . . my life crashed down round my ears and . . . you don't even tell me that she –

Wilby   Got to get the facts.

Delroy   This how you normally do things?

Karn *has entered: he has a cup of coffee.*

Karn   Normally do things?

Delroy   He's . . . asking all these fucking stupid questions and –

Karn   Procedure. Procedure. You did not deviate from procedure, Mister Wilby?

Wilby   No, sir.

Karn   Quite. We have procedures Mister Delroy. They change, from time to time. Orders from the top.

Wilby *gets up and stands.* **Karn** *sits.*

He lights a cigarette.

From the very top. A word in the ear. Commissioner. The top cop. The Home Secretary has a word in his ear and it's passed down, right along the line. The actual texture of the force changes. From government to government. You see, Mister Delroy. Tonight it's . . . unusual. We're in a state of chassis tonight. At a kind of crossroads. It really does seem as though tomorrow we shall have a new government.

Wilby   Really?

Karn   ITN still reckoning on a 65 per cent majority.

Wilby   Oh bugger.

Karn (*confidentially, to* **Delroy**)   He's got money on it, the result.

Delroy   I don't give a fuck about nothing except my –

Karn   It's related, Mister Delroy! (*Slight pause.*) Related to your predicament. You see, perhaps this will prove to be the first investigation, the first case to climax under the new regime. Requiring different perspectives.

Wilby   He couldn't remember the date of the birth of his eldest child.

Karn   Well, you see, there you are. Depending upon the swing of the pendulum. In the old days . . . in the old days until quite recently we'd have had to have said: Our poor old coloured friend here. What could be more natural in the world, the pressures he's under, the miseries of his wretched life on the very bottom rung of society's ladder, we must try to understand, poor chap. (*Pause.*) But . . . I sense the sands are shifting. I think, Mister Delroy, all these

fucking bleeding-heart social workers are for the high jump.
I think we might find ourselves on firmer ground where we
behave as policemen instead of crutches and we ask:

Karn *shouts loudly.*

What do you mean you don't fucking know when the
bastard you're getting child allowance for was born? I bet
you fucking remember when you go for the fucking state
handouts.

Pause. **Karn** *smokes his cigarette. In a quiet voice.*

I mean, they may be our new orders from the top. To
toughen up, a touch. And Mister Delroy, believe me . . .
after what some of us have endured in the name of equality
. . . and freedom . . . and civil liberties . . . and racial
harmony and all that . . . bullshit . . . it will make a nice
change. To start coming to terms with the realities of these
diseased, disgusting days . . . you know?

Pause.

I think it's on the cards, actually. I think. I think the beloved
Thatch isn't quite the soft touch she's reckoned to be. In
fact, a little dicky bird whispered to me that she is an
admirer of policemen. That she sees we may be required for
the struggle ahead . . . to the tune of a forty per cent pay
rise. Well, I mean. One doesn't fart about with that kind of
money unless one means to flex the muscles it is feeding.

Pause.

Perhaps I'm jumping the gun.

Wilby   I think you are, rather.

Karn   Am I?

Wilby   There's a long way to go.

Karn   Quite right.

Wilby   A long night ahead.

Karn   Yes.

Wilby   A lot can happen.

Karn   Indeed. A cup of coffee, Mister Delroy?

Slight pause.

Get him a cup of coffee, Mister Wilby. And a Club biscuit.

Wilby *goes, closing the door.*

Pause.

Karn   Mister Wilby, I thought he ought to go and
cool down. I forgot, forgot his point of view. I don't
want to over-excite him. You see . . . there's been a bit of
tragedy in his life. He took it most badly. He couldn't
unburden it, couldn't tell anyone. He's unlike us. Unlike
you and me Mister Delroy. He's not a family man.
Now take me for instance. When I get upset about
something. I have a wife to go home to. I can shed the
labours and the anxieties of the day in conversation with my
wife, across the supper table. She has quite a repertoire of
continental dishes, picked up on our travels. Now our
children are off our hands, we have time and the extra
finance for travelling, abroad. We have become quite jet-
setting on our packages. We might pop over to California in
the autumn to visit an aunt on my wife's side. Freddie Laker
has done a great deal for people like us. We buy
Linguaphone records and cassettes for each other at
Christmas, so that we can learn a phrase or two in the native
tongue of the country we shall visit in the summer. To
enable us to talk to the locals, an exchange of views and
customs. My wife and I frequently converse over the
telephone in foreign languages. I ask her what she's cooking
for supper in Spanish and she enquires after my work in
French or Greek. Oh yes. That's the difference between
Wilby and me. Between him and you. He has no family life.
He is alone. He has no wife.

Delroy   My wife, she died tonight.

Pause.

My wife and the child she was carrying.

Karn   About her pregnancy –

Delroy   They're both dead. I . . . I . . . well . . .

Delroy *shivers.*

Karn   I do understand. I want to help you.

Pause.

Help you . . . get it off your chest. But, first we just have to get these things down, the basics. Now, we haven't even got your address here.

Delroy   He said . . . said she was killed.

Karn   Oh yes.

Delroy   Murdered.

Karn   Indeed, someone caused her death.

Delroy   Who?

Karn   Who? What do you mean, who?

Delroy   Who did it?

Karn   Eh?

Delroy   Why –

Karn   Why?

Delroy   Whoever –

Karn   Come off it old son. I mean . . . what the fuck do you think we brought you in here for?

Delroy   Oh, ah, no.

Karn   Your address?

Delroy   Oh God. Jesus, Jesus, Jesus. You think . . . ? I weren't even there after . . . when . . . from after seven . . .

Karn   There is no necessity for the person responsible for the death to be with the victim at the time of the victim's last breath.

Delroy   Jesus Christ.

Karn   On the contrary, in my experience of twenty-seven murders, the killer very rarely has been on the scene unless it was he who called us to confess. And invariably they're domestics. Husband and wife dos. Oh, of course . . . you never called, did you?

Delroy   I was –

Karn   It was the doctor on casualty at the hospital who called, yes.

Delroy   You think . . . you think . . .

Karn   I never speculate. I have hunches, intuitions. I check the facts in a series of eliminations and I'm left with the . . . undeniable. Mostly, as I had suspected. So. You live at . . . ah, here it is . . . you've lived here how long?

Pause. **Delroy** *stands.*

Delroy   I demand to phone my solicitor.

Karn   You what?

Delroy   You think . . . what you're saying . . . what you're inferring, yeah, what you're inferring . . . I demand to talk to my solicitor.

Karn   Why?

Delroy   I got rights. I know my rights. My right is to talk to my solicitor. I've been here nearly four hours and – let me go.

Karn   I can't do that.

Delroy   Then my rights is I can phone my solicitor.

Karn   Are you insisting on that?

Delroy You're dead right. I'm insisting. I'm insisting. It's my legal entitlement. I stand by my entitlements.

Karn I see. I thought, just the two of us, a cosy little chat –

Delroy I demand –

Karn All right!

Delroy *sits as* **Karn** *goes across to the phone and lifts the receiver.*

Send Wilby up. He's in the canteen. Pronto. There's a man here demanding his rights. (*Pause.*) Oh really! So how many's that they've lost now then? (*Laughs.*)

He replaces the receiver.

Of course, your rights . . . they might all be candyfloss come tomorrow, the new dawn.

Silence.

You could make it easy for yourself.

Delroy I'm not saying nothing until I've had my rights and that's it.

Karn I see. Man of your word are you?

Delroy I am.

Karn If you say something, you stand by it?

Delroy I do.

Karn So, if you told your wife she couldn't have another kid since you was on the breadline what with the 23 quid whatsit and . . . mm, that's interesting.

Karn *makes notes on his pad.*

Oh dear, oh dear.

Delroy What's the matter?

Karn I beg your pardon?

Delroy What are you writing down? What's that then?

Karn   I'm afraid I can't tell you Mister Delroy.

Delroy   But you –

Karn   Delroy, I don't think either of us had better say anything else until you've taken advice from your solicitor. Since things have now become . . . so unreasonably official. And I shall say nothing.

Delroy   I ain't saying nothing neither.

Karn   Right.

They stare at each other.

Then **Karn** *goes to the phone and dials.*

Bon soir, ma cherie. Ooo, je ne sais pas. Je crois, je crois . . . il n'est pas possible que j'arrive a la maison ce soir parce que j'ai . . . um . . . j'arrive pendant le matin, je crois. (*Aside to* **Delroy**.) My wife, she's preparing a French lunch for tomorrow. (*On the phone again.*) Tres bien, ma cherie. Au revoir.

He replaces the receiver.

Delroy   Look, what I'm saying is –

Karn   You want to say something now?

Delroy   Like I've . . . well, be reasonable, I've been here since –

He gestures at his watch.

Karn   I say, that's a nice watch. A very nice watch indeed. Not the sort of watch I'd have thought a man of your standing would –

Delroy   Is it a crime to wear a watch now?

Karn   Now, now. You're being hypothetical again, Mister Delroy. Is it an offence for you to be in possession of that watch, you enquire. I do not know. I can't know, until I have sifted the facts. I do not know. You'd be amazed, Mister Delroy, at the number of humdrum little things that

can be offences nowadays. It's . . . staggering. And there are
hundreds of new things every year. More and more things
for a copper to remember. They mount up. In some
countries, every few years they review their laws. Chuck out
all the old, useless, outdated laws to keep the overall total
down. It makes life a little easier for the law enforcement
officers. It has its faults of course. For example it makes it
difficult to know what procedure to follow should we
witness in East Ham High Street a crusader chopping the
head off a dragon. But by and large it's sensible policy.

Delroy   Listen, I –

Karn   Mister Delroy, you have posed a highly complex
fucking question and you shall hear a highly complex
fucking answer. I have intrigued and fascinated drinking
acquaintances in six Mediterranean resorts with this
fascinating catalogue of facts and never has one made an
excuse and left for whom English was his native tongue.
Given the state of things in English law, the refusal of
successive governments to withdraw the outdated laws even
after many centuries' disuse, we find ourselves in possession
of a compelling, mind-boggling catalogue of 'crimes'. You
moan and whine and whimper about sus and harassment by
the police, but by Christ, we could nail you any day of the
week for a galaxy of crimes, sunshine. Did you know, do you
know it is an offence for an Englishman over the age of
twelve not to practice archery on a Sunday? It is an offence.
I could pick you up any Sunday morning for not doing
your archery, Delroy.

Delroy   What you fucking talking about?

Karn   Henry the Fifth! Good King Harry. It was all his
doing. You know what he was like, after his victories at Crec
and Agincourt and . . . oh bugger . . . what was that other
place? Anyway, after his three unforgettable victories, won
by his archers, he did pass, by royal degree in the early
fifteenth century . . . ordered every man over the age of
twelve to practice archery for one hour every Sunday

morning and that law has never been repealed. Although, should I ever catch you with a bow and arrow on Wanstead Flats on a Sunday morning, Delroy, I'd do you for offensive weapons. Curious what?

Delroy   I –

Karn   You see, what this country needs is . . . a strong government to sort out the laws. Bring order.

Delroy   You're mad.

Karn   Someone up there is. Someone up there is round the fucking bend. Do you know it is still an offence to drop a hand-grenade out of a balloon? I kid you not, it is. OK to use napalm in Vietnam, but dropping hand-grenades out of balloons is a crime against humanity. According to the St Petersburg Conference of 1880.

Delroy   I –

Karn   I see I have intrigued you with my knowledge of history. Hated it at school, but now I can't read enough of the stuff. I'm a member of the History Book Club. It gives one a perspective on things.

Enter **Wilby**.

Wilby   Callaghan was on. He refused to comment. He looked very put out when they asked him to comment on the way it was going. They were routed in Angus South.

Karn   Mister Delroy has little interest in Angus South, but like Sonny Jim, he refuses to comment.

Wilby   Oh. Oh well, that make things a bit difficult.

Karn   We must behave according to the book, Wilby. Or he might complain to his MP.

Wilby   Way it's going, he'll have a different one tomorrow.

Karn   He's asked to phone his solicitor.

Wilby   What a bloody cheek.

Karn   I couldn't believe my ears.

Delroy   I know my rights.

Karn   Wilby, a word in your ear.

Delroy *remains seated at the table:* **Karn** *goes to the far corner of the room and whispers in* **Wilby***'s ear. They return to* **Delroy**.

Wilby   Right, empty your pockets.

Delroy   Eh?

Wilby   You've got to empty your pockets.

Delroy   I'm not saying nothing.

Karn   Do it without talking then.

Delroy   No.

Wilby   It's procedure, Delroy. It's your rights. There's a set of events which must be done in order before you get to your right to phone your solicitor. Before we can let you do that, you've got to empty your pockets.

Delroy   I never knew that.

Karn   Look on it as an education then.

Pause. **Delroy** *rises and begins to empty his pockets.*

Karn   Write this down. One packet of cigarette papers.

Wilby   One packet cigarette papers.

Karn   Half ounce Old Holborn.

Wilby   Half ounce Old Holborn.

Karn   Three keys on ring.

Wilby   Three keys on ring.

Karn   Fifty pence in coins.

Wilby   Fifty pence.

Karn   In coins, as opposed to notes. And three pound notes.
In wallet. One underground train ticket dated February 12ᵗʰ
value 60p. One airmail letter postmarked Trenchtown. One
. . . photo. One comb containing hair. One almost empty
packet of cheese biscuits. And give us the watch. One watch.

Pause.

Anything else?

Delroy   No.

Karn   Right then, Delroy. Dial nine for a line.

Delroy *dials nine.*

Got the line? Then you may speak to your solicitor.

Delroy *stands holding the receiver.*

Wilby *is reading the airmail letter;* **Karn** *reads over his shoulder.
He looks at the motionless* **Delroy**.

Something the matter?

Delroy   I err . . .

Karn   Line all right?

Delroy   It's . . . um.

Karn   Come on Delroy, get on with it. All the fuss and
aggravation you've caused, demanding your rights. Wilby
here missed his supper break.

Delroy   It's just that . . . err.

Pause.

I ain't got a solicitor.

Pause.

I err . . . I don't exactly know any solicitors.

Karn   You don't have to play gold with them. You just have
to ring one up, them's your rights.

Delroy   There was one I talked to at the Law Centre.
I don't know the number. Do you know their number?

Karn   No.

Delroy   See I . . . what do I do then?

Karn   Do?

Delroy   I want to talk to a solicitor.

Karn   You're asking me . . . *me* . . . what you should do?

Delroy   If you know a solicitor . . . ?

Karn   I know dozens.

Delroy   I'd be very grateful if . . . if you'd err . . .

Karn   What?

Delroy   If you'd tell me one's name. So I would phone him
up, if you know his number.

Pause

Karn   (*to* **Wilby**) Did you hear that? (*To* **Delroy**.) Tollerton
Davies and Judd.

Delroy   Thank you. Do you, um, know the number?

Karn   544 2837

Delroy   Thank you.

Delroy *dials it. On the last digit.* **Karn** *says:*

Karn   Mister Delroy, that is their office number. And it is
now two o'clock in the morning.

Pause. **Delroy** *very slowly replaces the receiver and leans against
the wall.*

Delroy   That's err . . . personal. What you're looking at.

Karn   Who is this?

Delroy   The photo?

Karn Who?

Delroy   That's a photo of Georgie.

Karn   Your wife?

Delroy   Yes.

Karn   Who died tonight?

Silence.

This is a letter from her then?

Delroy   Yes.

Karn   She wrote you a letter?

Delroy   Yes. Sir.

Silence.

Karn   What's she doing writing you a letter then?

Delroy   It was . . . some years ago.

Wilby   From Trenchtown?

Delroy   She went there, with the baby.

Wilby   Went back to Trenchtown. Why?

Karn   Holiday?

Delroy   Well . . .

Karn (*to* **Wilby**)   How can that lot afford flights to fucking nig-nog land? Freddie Laker don't go there.

Delroy   We was . . . hmmm. (*Pause.*) Maybe gonna go back there. To live.

Pause. **Karn** *shows* **Wilby** *the letter.*

Wilby   She wasn't especially talented at writing letters, was she?

Delroy   It was the only one she ever wrote.

Karn To you.

Delroy I kept it.

Karn I can't read this scrawl.

Wilby A poem, is it? Is it a poem?

Delroy I missed her, when she went there.

Wilby By there, you mean Trenchtown?

Karn You was thinking of going back home then? Pity you didn't.

Delroy We talked about it . . . the circumstances here. The job. It was in Sudbury. I had to get up at four o'clock in the morning . . . and walk for miles . . . to the work coach and –

Karn You should have gone back. Back home.

Delroy Then we . . . had another baby. Coming. So, to make a life here . . .

Karn So your missus went to sort out the possibilities?

Delroy Yeah. She liked the idea. We was saving up. For four and a half years.

Karn She come back?

Delroy Then she had another baby.

Pause.

Karn You must have been pleased when she came back.

Delroy I lost the job. Never the money, like . . .

Karn This a poem then? She wrote poetry then?

Delroy Nar, a song. She thought I'd miss her when she went back. I did. The week before she went . . . we went to see this concert. At the Lyceum, Marley, he singed it. Her name in the song, and her going back, like . . . so it was her song . . . to me . . . and to her . . .

Karn *reads from the letter approaching* **Delroy**.

He stands beside **Delroy**.

He reads the lyrics aloud in a flat voice.

Karn   No woman, no cry
  I remember when we used to sit
  In the government garden in Trenchtown
  That was a place of rest
  We would mingle with the good people we met
  Good friends we have, good friends we last –

Delroy   Good friends we *lost*,
  Along the way
  In the great future you can't forget your past
  So dry your eyes, I say
  No woman no cry
  Little darling, don't shed no tears
  I remember when we used to sit
  In the government garden in Trenchtown
  And then Georgie would make a fire alight
  So it was wood smoke burning through the night
  So it was wood smoke burning through the night
  Then we would go into the forest
  For things I share with you
  My feet are my only carriage
  'Cause I've got to push on through
  But what I'm gonna believe is
  Everything is going to be alright.
  Everything . . .
  Is going to be alright.

Silence. **Karn** *sits.*

Karn   But it's not all right is it?

Pause.

You should have cleared out Delroy. When you had the chance. Oh, I wouldn't like to be a nigger in the new England. Yesterday they voted for the price of bacon and a tanner off your tax. They talked about supermarkets and jobs. They never mentioned what was going to happen to the likes of dole scroungers like you. There won't be no protection now. I think the results tonight prove everybody's got a bit sick of all that. Sick of civil fucking liberties, and Anti Fucking Nazi League having riots in our decent streets and thousands of honest cops having to be dragged out to stop fucking Yids and Pakkis and Indians and God-knows-who bashing hell out of half a dozen stupid, inarticulate red-necked Fascists. They got sick all right. They got so sick they had to form a Special Force, a Special Patrol Group. It's all trained up. Waiting for the order. I think things are going to be different from now on Delroy. I think you lot step over the mark from now on and there'll be no fucking dole, mate – just a one-way ticket home.

Delroy   Racist pig.

Karn   I was hoping you were going to be able to resist using that insult, Mister Delroy. It has the effect of bringing back some unfortunate memories for Mister Wilby here. Doesn't it Wilby?

Wilby   It does indeed.

Karn   Tell him what happened.

Wilby   I'd rather not.

Karn   Mister Wilby, that is an instruction.

Wilby   There was a riot. And err . . . in the bustle . . . the demonstrators . . . they . . . were kicking us . . . and when we defended ourselves, they screamed – when the television cameras were on them – they screamed: Racist pigs, Fascist pigs. Do I have to continue, sir?

Karn   Tell him. Tell him what it was like before the Special Patrol Group.

Wilby   We . . . we were unprotected. I was kicked harshly in the genitals. Rusty, my dog, he went berserk and chased the demonstrator. To his house. I was on the end of the lead in pain. Rusty chased him up the stairs. But he opened the door of his room and slammed it shut hard. Crushing Rusty's skull in the gap.

Pause.

I was powerless to help. Rusty's head was smashed tight in the closed door. The demonstrator was too afraid to open it; the dog screamed in agony. He . . . the youth inside the room . . . reached out and took a weighing machine . . . a heavy old weighing machine . . . and repeatedly struck Rusty over the head. Crushing the skull. Until he died.

Pause.

I thought that was extremely cruel. To do to a dog.

Delroy   Yeah, sure, but . . . I don't know what any of this has to do with me.

Karn   Tonight your wife died in highly suspicious circumstances. She was found in enormous pain and screaming out and bleeding like a soda fountain.

Wilby   On the bedside table were pills. Like a chemist's shop.

Delroy   I got them for her.

Karn   When?

Delroy   She was having a lot of pain last night.

Karn   A lot?

Delroy   Yes. She had a lot about six months ago. Belly aches. We went up to the hospital. This was when we found out she was pregnant.

Karn   Didn't you know?

Delroy   I didn't like to think about it.

Karn   Didn't you know?

Delroy   I didn't like to think about it.

Karn   Why not?

Delroy   When she said she'd missed a period, well, the thought of another kid . . .

Slight pause.

Karn   I understand.

Wilby   His rooms are really quite frightful. They smell. The whole house smells of Jeyes Fluid.

Karn   I understand you'd have wanted to end the pregnancy.

Delroy   She didn't believe in that.

Karn   Morally?

Wilby (*looks at the photo*)   She doesn't look a very moral woman. She wears false eyelashes.

Karn   I believe you. Is that why you never went to a doctor about a legal abortion?

Delroy   I went to the doctor for something for her pain.

Karn   When?

Delroy   This morning.

Karn   It was bad again this morning?

Delroy   It was terrible this morning.

Karn   You spent three fucking hours in the pub.

Delroy   She was all right after I went to the doctor this morning.

Karn   You went to the doctor?

Delroy   Yeah, I'm telling you –

Karn   Your wife was in pain, so you went to the doctor. If she'd had toothache, would you have gone to the dentist?

Delroy   She couldn't walk for pain.

Karn   What time did he visit her?

Delroy   He didn't visit her.

Karn   Why not?

Delroy   He said it wasn't necessary.

Karn   She's dead.

Slight pause.

Delroy   I asked him to come. But he said . . . said it was the baby, the time she'd been pregnant, he said it was normal sometimes.

Karn   He doesn't sound a particularly conscientious doctor.

Wilby   Not white.

Karn   His name?

Delroy   I don't know.

Karn   Don't know the name of your own doctor?

Delroy   I can't pronounce it.

Karn   So you just left it at that then?

Delroy   He gave me some pills. I mean, he give them for her.

Karn   And?

Delroy   I went to the chemist and got them. I mean, he'd gived me a prescription and I got them and . . . she took them. She was very hot.

Karn   You said she was shivering – you tried to mend the fire.

Delroy   She said she was shivering but she felt hot to me.

Karn   The pills, the pills –

Delroy   She took them. She said she felt a lot better. She had a kip. She was asleep. She was a lot better.

Karn   So you went to the pub?

Delroy   I weren't going to go. She wanted me to go.

Karn   And you went?

Delroy   Yes, sir.

Silence. **Karn** *paces, turns.*

Karn   At your flat, my chaps found: a screwdriver. It was long and thin and very bloody. Blood all over it. The same blood that was over the nightie and the sheets and the floor and –

Delroy   I was trying to mend the gas fire –

Karn   It was smothered in your wife's blood.

Delroy   Look, Jesus, don't keep going on about her bleeding and bloody, please. Have some fucking pity.

Karn   The casualty doctors, when they saw her, they knew right away. They phoned us up. They said: Someone's done an abortion on her. All the signs of interference. You did it. You fucking killed her. You left her to die while you went boozing in the pub.

Delroy   Lies, lies – fucking lies!

Karn   That poor woman . . . you wiped her out like this.

Karn *rips up the snapshot.*

Delroy   You fucking cunt –

Delroy *lunges at* **Karn**. **Wilby** *hits* **Delroy**. *He falls groaning.* **Karn** *crouches low beside him.*

Oh please . . . didn't mean . . .

Karn   Make it easy for yourself. Admit it now Delroy. Then we can all go home and watch the election results.

Pause. **Karn** *rises and goes to the door.*

Wilby, watch it.

Karn *goes.* **Wilby** *slowly helps* **Delroy** *up. Then repeatedly beats him in the guts.* **Delroy** *falls weeping and groaning.*

Blackout.

Music loud. Dylan's 'Baby Stop Crying' chorus.

Act Three

Music fades as the lights go up. **Delroy** *sits breathing deeply at the table: he's jacketless, his shirt open to the waist.* **Wilby** *comes in smoking and sipping coffee from a paper cup.*

Wilby   They're expecting Callaghan to resign at any minute. Thorpe lost Devon. He lost his seat. That put Mister Karn in very high spirits. He would be positively beaming if he hadn't had to hang around here all night. For you. He'll book you as soon as the post-mortem's come through. Not long now.

Delroy   Someone must help me.

Wilby   We'd call your GP, only you said you couldn't remember his name. I can't see any bruising. Mind you, it wouldn't show up any way, would it?

Delroy   This is a nightmare. This doesn't happen in England.

Wilby   It's been quite a time for you. One way and the other.

Delroy   My . . . children . . .

Wilby   I don't expect you'll be seeing them for quite a long time.

Delroy   I . . . there must be someone I can talk to.

Wilby   Everyone here is very annoyed with you. They think you're a savage doing what you've done. We appreciate your limited finances, but you can get abortions on the National Health.

Delroy   I never . . . never did it.

Wilby   Well, that's just not true.

Delroy   Love her, I do.

Wilby   Oh well. It takes all sorts.

Pause. **Karn** *enters with a plate of bacon sandwich. He sits.*

Karn   Has he made the confession?

Wilby   No.

Karn   Then fuck him. The minute the doctor rings, charge him and get him in Court at ten thirty. I want this case public today. The new dawn. Let them chew his bollocks off.

He looks at the sandwich.

This bacon is like old rope. (*He pushes the plate away.*) You should have gone to Trenchtown when you had the chance. It would have been different there. To where you're going. I don't know. I don't know why you didn't see the writing on the wall. How much dole did you say you get? Why the fuck should we be bled for the lives of you? What did you think it was going to be like when you came here?

Delroy   I was born here.

Karn   You're father weren't.

Delroy   Someone, somewhere in your family weren't.

Pause.

Karn   Skip reckons Keith Joseph will be Home Secretary. There's a no-nonsense man. He'll ship the lot of you home. Government will run for the five years – Thatch will be governor in 1984. There's a thought.

Pause. He lights a cigarette.

Are you a political man Mister Delroy?

Delroy   Yesterday I'd have said no. Today . . . it begins.

Karn   If there's a by-election you'll be able to stand as a candidate – since you're on a murder charge. There was an incident . . . refresh my memory Wilby. In the Job, I read it. Some prisoner, some nick . . . prisoner refused . . . they wouldn't let him play rugby. Rugby union for the prison team. He was a murderer too. Remember reading it

. . . the president of the rugby union federation, or whatever it was, said: there are no rules in rugby union preventing convicted murderers playing our game. But this man cannot play for the team because he has played rugby league. (*Laughs.*) I dunno . . . we're all barmy.

Wilby   Thorpe lost then?

Karn   You've lost your bet.

Wilby   Cabinet ministers have lost their seats.

Karn   No-one is safe from the Thatch.

The phone rings. **Wilby** *answers it.*

Wilby   Yes . . . yes? Now . . . all right . . .

He replaces the receiver.

The governor . . . he wants you.

Karn   I'm waiting for the post-mortem to –

Wilby   They rang him.

Karn   Well?

Wilby   He wants to see you.

Karn   Now?

Wilby   Urgently.

Karn   Fuck it. Wilby, entertain Mister Delroy.

Karn *goes. Pause.* **Wilby** *sits.*

Wilby   You look very subdued Mister Delroy. In reflective mood? If you had your time again . . . change things? Is that what you're thinking?

Delroy   I'm thinking . . . .

Pause.

Wilby   No children. Not get married?

Delroy   I'm thinking, the day when the white boss called me a lazy nigger . . . this white boss, in the factory, in Sudbury, he was so ignorant and I thought: Don't fight him, he's winding you up, let it go . . .

Wilby   Yes?

Delroy   I'm thinking I wish I'd kicked his fucking teeth down his throat.

Wilby   That wouldn't have achieved anything. Except the sack.

Delroy   I got the sack anyway. I would have felt better when you did me over . . . I would have dreamed I was doing it to you.

Pause.

I'm innocent.

Wilby   Sure.

Delroy   I didn't do it. I never did.

Karn *enters fast.*

Karn   He didn't do it.

Wilby   What?

Karn   Cock up, fucking doctors got it wrong. He never did it.

Wilby   But they said –

Karn   I know what they fucking said. They went straight to the governor to explain they made a mistake. Looked like what they said, but post-mortem revealed . . . (*He reads from the notes.*) It seems you're owed an apology Mister Delroy. Your wife died of an ectopic pregnancy (*Reads.*) There was a rupture in her fallopian tube. The foetus was stuck there. It was starting to grow there. Instead of in her uterus. The tube is the width of . . . a hair. The doctors said that accounts for the vast haemorrhage. He said that's why she

experienced some . . . discomfort . . . He said it seemed
definite, given the screwdriver all bloody and . . . a rare
complication . . .

Pause.

Blame the fucking doctors, don't blame me.

Delroy   No?

Karn   You can go.

Delroy   Go . . . just like that?

Karn   Far to go? Want a lift?

Delroy   I go on my own. My kids . . .

Wilby   If you'll ring social services, they'll know.

Pause.

Delroy   I'd like the pieces of the photo, the letter.

He's putting on his jacket.

Wilby   All your possessions. (*He takes the list.*) One packet
cigarette papers, half ounce Old Holburn, three keys on
ring, fifty pence, three pound notes in wallet, underground
train ticket dated February 12th value 60p, one letter
postmarked Trenchtown, one photo . . . one packet cheese
biscuits . . . one watch . . . Sign there.

Wilby *moves the possessions across the table to* **Delroy** *as
he signs.*

Delroy   I want to make a phone call.

Karn   To the social services?

Delroy   Yes.

Karn   Wilby get him the number.

Wilby   Yes.

Wilby *goes.*

Karn   You're not an unintelligent man, Mister Delroy. You can surely appreciate that given the circumstantial evidence, given the –

Delroy   Have I got to listen to you?

Karn   I don't want you getting . . . what happened . . . out of proportion.

Pause. **Wilby** *enters with a piece of paper.*

Wilby   Number here.

Karn   Mister Delroy, I wouldn't bother wasting your time and energies on any exaggerated heroic expectations. You're not a unique case. Let it be forgotten. I advise you very strongly, drop it.

Delroy *gobs in* **Karn**'s *face.*

Pause.

Karn *wipes the spittle from his face.*

Karn   Then Mister Delroy, let me bring you up to date with the reasons you were . . . unfortunately delayed here on the night your wife died. There were a number of breakings and enterings in your area. A witness saw someone leaving a premises. It could have been you. You have been here on suspicion of breaking and entering. But once we heard of your wife's tragic demise . . . we offered you comfort, took care of your children . . . and dropped all possible charges.

Pause.

Or better still, tell you what – I'll tell you why you were here tonight, Delroy. You were here on . . . sus.

Karn *and* **Wilby** *go, closing the door. Slowly* **Delroy** *pockets his possessions.*

Music fades in as the lights fade to blackout: Bob Marley's 'No Woman No Cry', loud.

End